MOTHERLESS CHILD

A Journey of Growing Up and Forgiving

By. Valencia Griffin-Wallace

Other Titles by The Author:

31 Days to Building Your BOLD Factor

Life Required

Co-Authored Titles:

Transition: Create the Life You Desire

Transition: Ashes Emanating Beauty

Unapologetically Winning

This is a work of creative nonfiction. The events are portrayed to the best of Valencia Griffin-Wallace's memory. While all the stories in this book are true, some names and identifying details have been changed to protect the privacy of the people involved.

ISBN-13: 978-0-692-06440-5
For Worldwide Distribution
First Printing, 2018
Printed in the United States of America

Motherless Child | 5

"A motherless child is something I never defined myself by.

How much or little I was defined by that title, I will never

know, since I can't picture a life other than the one I lived."

– Valencia G. Wallace

TABLE OF CONTENTS

DEDICATION

To the late Griezelda L. Jones, my mother. May you rest in

peace knowing your work has been published and your

talent acknowledged. Thank you.

Acknowledgements

Above, on the side and below everything else... I am

a Southern woman where thank you is a part of our culture.

With that being said, I must first and foremost thank the

queens who went before me, my great-grandmother,

Harietta, my grandmother, Jo Carolyn, and of course my

mother, Griezelda. As I look back on my life and theirs, I see

the strength and beauty were in my DNA.

Even though a queen can be complete without a

king, my king served as a catalyst for my purpose. David

Wallace, my husband, is that prayer I didn't know I prayed.

Having a husband that is also your best friend is a woman's

dream. From day one, you have given my strength, wiped

tears, and motivated me beyond words. I look forward to

growing old with you and enjoying the harvest of the seeds

we have planted in each other.

Kamrin, mama's Rock Star, mama's rock! Your birth

truly gave me a reason to live. Your presence in my life

served as a constant reminder that I can do something right.

You are love in the truest form. Thank you for being a part

of me and being mama's biggest cheerleader. I hope to

make you proud.

Author's Note

This is the story of my life, wherein some names and events have been changed; it is a work done in truth from a place of forgiveness. Memories are no respecter of time and seem to happen as our brain chooses to deliver them.

Writing this was an unexpectedly emotional journey for me. I started ten years ago and then started over in 2017. Why start over when it was already done? I was in a different place in my life's journey. Now I have a better understanding of the hurt and pain my mother carried until the day she died. Well, as much as one could understand from reading old journals and spiral notebooks she left behind.

Now I wonder, did she really even have a chance? At an early age, her childhood innocence was taken from her. The things that happened in her life after that were a mixture or "gumbo" if you will, of chaos, family drama, and personal demons that drove her to the crack house.

Griz, as everyone called her, was different from the rest of the family. Outspoken, outgoing, and fully aware of her beauty, she used those things to her advantage. Men fell at her feet and to this day memories of her still haunt them. She was a fighter, she was a lover, she was a mom, she was a creative soul who loved to sew and write, but most of all, she was a woman tormented. No matter how much she loved her girls, she still longed for the son she lost two years before my birth in 1977. As you read the words in her poetry, it screams of a woman heartbroken and searching for something. Her unfulfilled search led her down a dark path and then to an untimely, unsolved murder in 1994.

As her oldest daughter, I was blessed to have her talents and cursed to live in my own torment until I released her from my expectations. My life seemed to be going along the same path as hers. I suffered similar trauma, robbed of my childhood by a relative and later by mom's drug abuse. Before I went down the all too easy spiral of losing myself, I had my son and realized I had a purpose. This story is part of it.

Addiction doesn't just affect the addicts; it affects everything around them. As society mocks them and share videos of "crackheads" doing crazy things in public, who stops and wonders where their children are? No one! My story and the story of countless other nameless, faceless but no less... Motherless Children had to be told. Her drug addiction was the catalyst that put me on the path of my

purpose and the path to tell her story.

MOTHERLESS

CHILD

FOREWORD

The subject addressed in this book will probably affect every person reading it at some point in their lives. Whether it is a family member, friend, co-worker, or simply the clerk you see at your local grocery store, everyone knows or is related to someone struggling with or recovering from substance abuse. It is not always easy to tell your real story – the one where things are far less than perfect, and life is not so rosy and bright. People may know you from our social media profile and all of the photos posted on our timeline, but that doesn't mean they know the real you. It becomes even more difficult to share when your story contains tragedy and disappointment. There is no greater heartache than when a child experiences the loss of a parent because of addiction. In her book "Daring Greatly: How the Courage to Be Vulnerable Transforms the Way We Live, Love, Parent, and Lead", Brene Brown states "Because true belonging only happens when we present our authentic, imperfect selves to the world, our sense of belonging can never be greater than our level of self-acceptance." Valencia Griffin Wallace has finally come to the point of self-acceptance, and it comes across clearly in this book. She is a contrast against the backdrop of her own struggle and pain. She is a Survivor and more than that she is a conqueror. I have witnessed her rise above the circumstances that could have placed her right in the middle of the same scenario that her mother struggled with. She is one of those rare individuals who decided to become the master of her own fate and overcome the odds.

She has never been content to settle, and she is always willing to dare. Not only does she speak from experience, but she also speaks from her heart as her story unfolds on the pages of this book. For all of the little children who go to bed at night in the homes of foster parents and strangers. For all of the mothers who have lost custody of their children because they cannot get a grip on the foul demon of addiction. This story serves as a reminder that your future is not determined by your DNA. It is determined by your level of hunger and desire to overcome. I am deeply touched by the courage and tenacity of this author. I can say beyond a shadow of a doubt that I have a deeper level of respect now that I have read this portion of her story. Now that she is on the other side looking back I Can Only Imagine the emotions she must have experienced while we are opening old wounds. Now that the work has been done and this book has been printed many will benefit from the wisdom contained in these pages. It is not simply a vehicle

for entertainment. The bonus of this material is its ability to

make you experience a range of emotions. You will laugh,

cry, feel joy and sadness as you see through the eyes of a

motherless child who took her story and made it into a

beautiful tapestry of life.

Paula McDade, CEO - Stellar Creative LLC

Editor-in-Chief, Brilliant Awakening Magazine

PROLOGUE

"Parents who do drugs, have kids who do drugs. Any questions?" That commercial played during Saturday morning cartoons. Every Saturday! If you grew up in the 80s, you either were on drugs or knew someone on drugs. It was the time of the "Drug-Free America" campaign. Commercials popped up like hotcakes letting all "us" children know if our parents did drugs, we were next! But we still shouldn't do them. According to the commercials, I was next in line since my mom was an addict. Boy, talk about generational curses.

Mom smoked weed, and even though at seven, I didn't exactly know what it was, I knew it was a drug. Crack was different. I wasn't sure what that was either, but I knew it wasn't weed.

Weed made her laugh and sleep; crack made her disappear. She disappeared into the bathroom; she disappeared at night; mom just started disappearing.

Curiosity had me. Following her out of the house was not an option, I had a baby sister and step-sister to watch over. The bathroom was another story. I could at least go into the bathroom and see what was going on in there.

Going in one day right after she came out, the smell hit me. It stunk and made my eyes burn. Nothing looked out of place, except the substance that was on the bathroom counter. Being seven and curious enough to taste it, I licked my finger. Feeling funny both physically and emotionally, the realization hit me. Mom was on drugs. Real drugs, the kind we learned about in school. So now, I was the parent.

It wasn't always like this. Once upon a time, I had a family with a dad who loved me and a mom who enjoyed life. I was a daddy's girl, and in my eyes, daddy couldn't do any wrong. We lived on a Navy base in California and mom was a housewife. She still got dressed up, did her hair and makeup, but never really went anywhere.

Watching her burn the tips of her wooden black eyeliner pencil, I didn't understand how she didn't burn her eye. I did understand and pray one day to be that beautiful. Mom was young, probably too young to have two kids and a man that was gone all the time. Dad would be gone on long trips on the Navy boat, but when he came home, life was happy. At least for us kids.

Mom was fun and outgoing, being locked down in a marriage with two kids at 20 years old was probably not the life she imagined. She felt imprisoned and lonely. Like I said earlier, all dressed up and no place to go until he came along. My dad left an opening that was perfect for someone else to sneak into our lives. The man with the black Camaro.

Dee was tall, dark, but far from handsome unlike my dad. He was weird and had a sneaky smile. He reminded me of one of those kids who did stuff but blamed it one somebody else. You always knew it was them though, the look on their face said it all.

He had a black Camaro, which I thought he was way too tall for. But I had to admit, it was a cool looking car even if I didn't like him. Dad would leave one day, Dee would pull up the next. Mom would pack us up in his car and we would ride to the park on base.

Noni, my baby sister played with his daughter like she didn't have a care in the world. I didn't blame her, at least she had someone to play with. Being older by one year, we didn't have much in common, plus she was a crybaby.

I didn't play on anything at the park. Somebody had to keep watch on what mom was doing with this strange man. Too young to quite understand what was going on, but old enough to know it wasn't right. My thoughts didn't matter, I was a child, what did I know? So, I just sat and glared at them not caring if they saw me. This was wrong and we all knew it, I just hoped my dad didn't find out. Months later, he did. One of the nosy Navy wives who lived by us, told her husband who blabbed to my dad. Listening with my ear to the door, I heard my dad yelling and my mom crying. Two sounds I never heard before and I knew nothing would be the same from that point on. Dad was hurt, and mom was the one who did it.

Next thing I knew, we were sent to stay with our family in Louisiana while they worked things out. The working things out part made me happy, going back to Louisiana didn't. I hated Louisiana. We sometimes went to visit when things were "funny" between my parents.

My family in Louisiana was different. They made us go outside and even gave us dumb rules to follow. Sometimes there would be threats like "you are going to get a whipping," but I would always call my dad's mom. We didn't get whippings; my parents didn't do that.

There was also another reason I hated Louisiana. My mom's brother was a pervert. He liked me to sit on his lap and I could feel his "thing." Sometimes, if I was laying down, he would touch me. They made us take naps, but I never went to sleep, just played sleep. No one said it out loud, but they all knew what he was doing.

We were kids, but we had to protect ourselves and not be "womanish." No wearing dresses without shorts, no twisting our hips when we walked, nothing to "entice" grown men to look at you. "Don't y'all go in that back room with him," we were told, and we better had listened.

I could never sleep there and often found myself staying up watching television until it went off. My aunts would go out and party knowing full well I would be up to let them back in.

Many sleepless nights went on at my grandmother's house. Partially wondering about what was going on with my parents, the other part listening for his footsteps.

One night, I was up watching scary movies. Of course, everyone else was sleep and wrapped up tight in the pallet we made on the floor. The pervert wore slippers and I could hear him sliding into the den. I prayed he just peeped in and went on about his business. No such luck.

Peeping out of one eye and playing sleep, I thought he would leave us alone. But he didn't. He leaned his stinky body over me and started rubbing my chest. I don't know why he picked me that night. Maybe because I was closest to the door. Maybe it was just my night.

He rubbed and rubbed on my chest like he expected a boob. Nothing was there, I was a kid. Too young to have even a little bit. This was going to end tonight though.

Sometimes, in certain situations, you hear a voice telling you to do something crazy. Well, my inner voice told me to say something. I was scared, and he was an adult. What was I going to say? Did it matter?

Let me try something else, I said to myself. I attempted to roll over like I was starting to "wake" up. Instead of it spooking him off, he just rolled me right back. My throat was dry as I started to say something. First attempt, nothing came off. I don't even think my mouth moved, but then a voice came out that I never heard.

"If you touch me, I will tell my dad." Now I didn't know if I still had a dad since mom messed up, but I knew this would scare him. My dad was known for fighting and anyone who knew him, knew he didn't play behind his G Baby (his nickname for me). He looked at me. "What you said guh?" "Guh" was the southern word for girl or gal, basically putting you back in a child's place.

My voice trembled, I was scared, but I said it again. "I. WILL. TELL. MY. DAD. And he will kill you." This time I was louder. If it didn't scare him off, someone would hopefully wake up. Silence, a look, and then he left. That was the last time he ever did that... to me.

A few months and many sleepless nights later, we were headed back to Cali. I could have Crip-walked the whole way, but that dance wasn't out then. Not wanting to mess things up, if my parents were back together, I didn't mention the pervert. Plus, I didn't want my dad going to jail because of me.

I felt like a dark cloud had been lifted, on to find myself in a middle of a hurricane. My parents were supposed to work things out and now our family would be back to normal. Instead, we came back to California and had a new "daddy." There were no questions to be asked because no answers would be given.

Dad was out, and Dee was in. Dee, the tall, dark-skinned man with the black Camaro. The man who took us to the park. The man who made mama smile. The man who took my daddy's place.

We were on a whole new base. Now, I had two sisters, Noni and Dee's daughter. They wanted us to just adjust. Kids are resilient and have short term memories, right? Wrong. I wanted my daddy! I said it every day. I said it to mom. I said it when I talked to dad on the phone. Everyone was going to know, I did not like this new family. Mom didn't pay attention to my wants, she was living a fairytale with her new husband.

The fairytale didn't last long though. Once Dee got comfortable, the real him eventually showed up. He didn't like me and eventually stopped trying to hide it. My looks, my DNA nor my parent's divorce were my fault, yet I was suffering for it. He treated Noni like she was his, but I was the "difficult" one. The outsider. Mom acted like she didn't notice what he did and how he treated me. She always reminded me "G, baby, be good", but that wasn't going to happen. I was mad at her and mad at Noni who was loving her new role as being a big sister.

Dee was outright mean. If I got an outfit from my dad, I was fat. If I made a mistake, I was stupid. If I played in makeup, I looked ugly. My mother tried to combat this with "motherly" words of love, but it wasn't enough. She needed to leave him and there was nothing else acceptable to me. Was she choosing him over me? Did she not see how he acted towards me? Even though he reserved his "stabbing" comments for when she wasn't around, she still knew.

I knew the things he said weren't true, but when you hear something long enough it starts to saturate your mind. My sister was pretty because she had "good" hair and was nice, my step sister was pretty because she was mixed. There was no "pretty" left for me. Plus, I was knock-kneed and awkward, things he made sure he pointed out, which added to my low self-esteem.

Their family was happier without me and I felt like an outsider. I wanted my old family back, but dad was off somewhere living a life without us. He had moved on and started a new family with some other woman.

By the time 4th grade rolled around, the school had implemented the D.A.R.E program. Drug Abuse Resistance Education, to teach us how to *resist* drugs, I guess. Most kids were in awe and confused that people did drugs. I knew the realities of it. My mom was on drugs. I didn't need their "candy coated" drug lessons. If anything, I could teach them the real deal.

They didn't have to worry about me ever doing drugs, but I did have questions. What do you do when your parent is the one doing drugs? Do you turn them in? Do you ignore the problem and pray it goes away? Why weren't they teaching that part? In 4th grade, I'm sure most of us weren't on drugs so how was this lesson relevant? It seemed like they weren't taking it seriously. I hated my classmates with their happy life and normal parents.

When we had lessons on sexual abuse, they

took it seriously. We all knew good touches and bad touches. At that point, it had been drilled in our heads. "No one touches your private parts. If they do, tell someone."

If you were touched, you were supposed to go to a parent, teacher, and cop to tell them. Even though that lesson was constantly taught, when I was molested I didn't tell anyone, I confronted the pervert and stopped it. That is how I was, always having to take care of things myself. Even then.

All that bravery I had, didn't apply to dealing with my mom. I wanted to scream at the instructors teaching the class. *SAVE ME, SAVE MY SISTER, PLEASE SAVE MY MOM!* But I didn't. I sat back in class, swallowed my tongue and my thoughts. There was no way I was going to tell them, so they can put us in an orphanage and my mom in jail. So, I didn't say anything. Ever.

During this time, I got in trouble at school. A lot. I didn't bully other kids, but if they pushed a button or annoyed me, they were going to get it. Going to the principal's office was my trip of the day most of the time. no one noticed how tired I was. No one noticed that I didn't pay attention in class. No one noticed anything except me being bad.

I didn't care about school and their dumb lessons anyway. They couldn't help me. The only lessons I needed to remember was the ones that kept us safe. I learned how to pretend an adult was home when we were there by ourselves. I also learned how to pretend like that I have a normal life while mom was off getting high. Most of all, I learned that I could hate someone and love them at the same time.

It hurt to admit that truth. I hated my mother, but I loved her too. Ouch! I blamed her for cheating and breaking up our family. I blamed her for bringing Dee into our happy picture, leaving my dad and then marrying him. I blamed her for partying and doing drugs, be happy and doing drugs, disappearing and doing drugs.

It was all her fault. Why wasn't she strong enough to just say no like the commercial said? Didn't she see my baby sister and I needed her to be in her right mind or was she just being selfish? Yes, I blamed her for a lot.

According to some messed up statistics I read, children of drug addicts have trust issues, are disconnected, show limited remorse, and little to no empathy. I see that in my own life, but I will do one better and add the limited capability to have healthy relationships.

Motherless child is not only my story, but the story of so many other motherless children. Society focuses on the drug addict and curing them while ignoring the destruction ingrained in those raised by them. We see the effects in criminals and the ones who became drug addicts, but there are some of us that wanted to fight for better life.

No one came to save me, I had to save myself or statistically, I was doomed. Motherless child is a journey of growing and forgiving my mother. At the end, that was my saving grace.

Chapter 1 -Addiction Survival Mode

I wanted to call my dad and tell him what was going on, but I knew I wasn't supposed to do that. So, I didn't. He should have known anyway. Isn't that what father's do? Know when their children are in harm's way? Pretty sure living with my mom and Dee was considered harm's way. No one sent him the memo and we were screwed.

It was Saturday, only the girls and I were home. Mom had left the night before and hadn't come back yet. The day came and went with no mom, but most of all no food. They often left us alone with an empty refrigerator. At that point, I had gotten used to being hungry and just dealing with it.

Today was different though. Noni and my step sister were in their room playing and watching Saturday morning cartoons. Hearing them in the hall walking towards me, I looked up from the kitchen table. "We hungry," Noni said. Giving her that "what the heck am I supposed to do?" look wasn't an option. I was the big sister and I was supposed to take care of her. That was the one thing both of my parents stressed.

But, there was nothing in the kitchen, both of us knew that. I went through the motions and opened it up anyway. Nothing except nasty bologna. It was Dee's bologna, so we weren't allowed to touch it. There was nothing else.

Frustrated, I slammed the refrigerator door and shooed them off. I had to think, which is not an easy task when you are hungry. "You guys go in the room and play." They needed to eat, and I was more concerned for them than me. I could always go to my friend's house and eat.

The role of a big sister or parent was one that was too big for me to fill, but if I didn't take care of her, who would?

Sitting at the kitchen table, I started to pray and silently cry. They were angry tears and I didn't know why I was praying anyway. God seemed to ignore my prayers of my parents getting back together. I didn't understand. *Where was mom? Why didn't my dad come and save us?*

Quickly wiping away tears before the girls walked back in the kitchen, I knew I had to be strong. No matter what, I could not let them see me cry. They trusted me to take care of them and if they saw me crying, that would be gone.

My thoughts were interrupted by the buzzer from the dryer. They liked the feeling of the warm clothes and normally would rush in to get them. I guess they were too busy playing because they didn't come in. Instead, I got the clothes out of the dryer. That was part of my chores anyway.

As I pulled out the clothes, I saw Dee's work uniform. I almost left them there, but something told me to pull them out. So, I did. Suddenly, dollar bills started coming out of the dryer mixed up in the clothes. The more clothes I pulled out, the more money came out. Did God hear me this time? I hit the lottery. It wasn't a lot of money, but enough to get us something to eat.

Smiling, I held the money tightly in my hand. Grabbing my jacket, I hollered to the girls. "You guys

stay here, I will be back with food." There was a PX, military store, around the corner.

The lady behind the counter eyeballed me when I walked in. She probably thought I was going to steal something or wondering why a little kid was in the store that time of night by herself.

Rice and hotdog wieners was all I needed to make a meal. They liked rice, butter, and sugar with fried wieners on the side. My mom had cooked it enough and by watching her, I knew I could do it too. Putting the food on the counter, the lady totaled it up. I still had some change left over. Grabbing some candy, I put it up there too.

Maybe it was the look in my eye. Maybe she knew something was wrong. It didn't matter, she bagged the stuff up, reached me the bag and my money back. "Whatever it is, you are going to be okay." She smiled, and I smiled back. I had food for my sisters and money. God really did see me. I wish I could say that was the last time we were left hungry, but it wasn't.

Chapter 2-Gang Life

When Dee's time was up, we were sent to a new base. Still in California, but a different part. We arrived in San Diego before the housing was ready and stayed at a hotel.

It was November 7th, my sister's birthday. She was jumping on the bed next to me, extra excited. I'm not sure what she was excited about, we were still living in a hotel. There was no one in the room except us kids, mom and Dee were gone.

At least they left a note this time. "We went to get something for your sister's birthday, be back. Love mom." Lies. I balled it up and threw the note in the trash. Noni was too busy jumping up and down on the bed screaming at the top of her lungs to notice their absence. "It's my birthday! It's my birthday!"

Hours later, her excitement started to die down, and reality was setting in. We were in a motel alone with no food on her birthday and then she said those dreaded words. "We hungry." Only this time there were no tears, no prayer and no dryer with money in it.

The anger started kicking in. I wasn't sure what *bullshit* was, but I was pretty sure this situation would fit. Going into the bathroom, I felt hot tears falling and wiped them away with the back of my hand. "Never let them see you cry." I heard my dad's voice in my head.

I was hungry too, but I couldn't let on. Brushing my teeth, the thought came to me that when I did that, I wasn't hungry. "You guys come in here." Like obedient little sisters, they came into the bathroom to see what I wanted. "Stick your finger out like this," I said pointing my finger at them.

When they did, I put toothpaste on it. "Now eat it." They looked at me questioningly, but they did as they were told. I didn't give them a lot, just enough to knock the edge off. The looks on their faces hurt me. I know it was disgusting, but they had to do it. That was all we had to eat.

About an hour later they were laying in the bed with stomach cramps. When mom and Dee finally came back, it was dark outside. "G made me eat toothpaste, and my stomach hurts," Noni said. Mom looked at me as she unpacked a bag of food.

"What was I supposed to do? You guys were gone, and they were hungry." Mom didn't say anything and instead handed Noni her birthday cake. That was it, nothing else was said. A few days later, we were moving into base housing.

The new base was different. The house was on top of a hill that had pickleweeds. Pickleweeds looked just like they sounded, weeds thick like pickles. I never saw them before, but I saw other kids sliding down them on cardboard boxes. I made a mental note to try that. The base was an "open" base. No MPs, military police, were guarding the base to keep the public out.

School was different too. It was year-round. It wasn't long before mom was back getting high. Going into 6th grade at a new school was not going to be easy, but I didn't care. Home was hard; school couldn't be worse than that.

School became an escape for me. The military base was in the middle of gang territory. Watching movies like

"Colors" and conversations with my mom, I knew what gangs were.

These weren't grown men running around shooting people; they were kids like me who just happen to be in a gang. They were Bloods and claimed the set of Bay View Posse. All the friends I hung with were in the gang. Gangs started young, and I knew I wanted to be part of it. Part of me wanted to join for them. You only could do so much hanging if you weren't in the gang. The other part of me wanted a family. Family meant protection.

They were the people who would look out for me and better yet, protect me from Dee who had started to get in my face.

By that time, he was fighting mom, and though I tried to stand up to him, it didn't do any good. She was slowly starting to wither away. She was giving up on life and us. He wasn't gone as much as she was and focused on making my life hell. The older I got, the more I looked like my dad and that bothered him more than anything else. Well, that and my refusal to call him anything but his first name. At least, I didn't call him homewrecker. To be honest, I didn't make it easy for them either. I was going through a rebelling stage and finally felt free.

It was a done deal. I was going to join. The days went by fast from when I made that decision. I thought my friend forgot to tell the heads that I was in until she gave me a note one day at school.

It was set up! One-day afterschool I would get "jumped in." Assuming and hoping my friends from school were going to do the deed, I wasn't worried. They would take it easy on me, plus I was a little bigger than them.

All day my friends kept asking me if I was scared. I wasn't. So much had happened in my life up until that point that fighting was nothing to me. I'd had fights and even stood up to my stepdad. If I was ready to dish out a lick or take a lick from him, why would I fear some girls?

Right after school, we headed to the baseball filed where it was supposed to go down. My nerves were starting to get the best of me. I didn't understand why I was nervous; it wasn't like they were going to kill me. Really, it didn't matter if I died though. Life was hell, and I was ready to leave.

When we got to the field, there were a bunch of high school kids and adults. I knew some of them from around the base. All of them had on gang colors: red, white, and black.

My friends left my side and went over by the high school girls. On my own and alone. I stood there; now I was scared. Nothing new, but this was different. This time I was fighting for a reason. No time for temporary fear when there is a bigger purpose in mind. And there was one. Joining the gang meant I was finally part of something. I wouldn't be the outsider anymore.

There was no bell, no "go" alert, nothing. I just got hit hard in the face. No time to think, all strategy out the window, it was do or die time. The hits were coming from everywhere, and only two things came to my mind. Protect my face and focus on what was in front of me. All the anger built up in my 6th-grade body from having a hard life was let out blow after blow. Rather, I held my own or not didn't matter at that moment; I just knew no matter what I wasn't going down.

There was no referee, no time limit, or limit on how many girls I was fighting. In my head, I just knew one thing I WILL NOT GO DOWN, and I didn't. Eventually, someone said, "That's enough," and the fight was over as quick as it started.

One of the older girls, who I later found out was one of the top people for BVP, handed me a red, white and black bandanna. I was in; I had earned their respect too. They had never seen someone so young hold their own like I did. Afterwards, we hung out at the park for a while, and then I went home. Even though, my body hurt, my lip was bleeding, and I was pretty sure I got hair pulled out, I was happy.

I remember on the walk home feeling pride. My walk was different, my head was held high, and I was on cloud nine. Kids looked at me with respect, adults... well not so much. It didn't matter, at the end of the day, I did what I set out to do.

Joining the gang changed me; I felt invincible. I knew after going through that I could handle just about anything. They taught me respect and pride. There was real love in my gang family.

Most weekends, we hung out on base or went to dances. Other times, we graffitied or *tagged* different buildings. Since I was an artist, I was one of the main taggers, and since I was good at fighting, I was one of the mains for that too.

Mom knew I was in a gang; my bandanna stayed with me. If I left the house, I repped or represented my set. Pretty soon all my clothes were red, white, and black. I loved gang life.

Besides graffiti, we didn't really do anything bad. We were base kids, with parents and curfews, but at the dances, we were all thugs.

They had more than one gang on the base, so dances were mostly filled with gang kids. Going to the dances, I knew not to dress up too much because we were going to fight. We protected each other when we fought because things would get crazy. You didn't know or care if you were fighting a guy or a girl, you just swung.

If we didn't get kicked out from the dance, it wasn't fun. We were kids playing adult games trying to escape the life our parents built. And like me, the rest of them didn't have ideal home lives either.

CHAPTER 3-READY FOR WAR

It was Sunday night and cool out. My friends were all at home eating family dinner. I was at home wondering where mom was. She had left the house earlier that day, taking my gold bracelet and my stereo to pawn. She said we needed food and they didn't have any money.

"Why is that my responsibility? I better get it back," I said with an attitude. Normally, mom would have said something, but she was too worried about getting high to deal with me. "You will." She lied and left out of the door.

Hours later, I smelled pizza. Leaving out the room, I walked into the kitchen expecting mom to be there. She hadn't returned yet and instead I found Dee, Noni, and my stepsister sitting at the table like a happy family eating.

"We got pizza," Noni said happily munching away with her mouth open. Walking over to the stove, I grabbed a plate.

Dee didn't say anything, but I could feel him watching me. I was hungry, and that was my only focus at that moment. "Before you eat my pizza, you need to wash those dishes in the sink." It wasn't my day to do the dishes, both he and I knew that. I didn't respond which made him mad. "Did you hear me?" His voice was loud and filled with disdain.

I still didn't respond as I sat down at the table with the plate in front of me. My sister stopped chewing and looked at me. Her eyes were pleading with me not to be difficult. She felt sorry for me, I think. Here I was her big sister who she loved, but I caused all the drama in the family. It didn't matter how she looked at me; I was going to eat or was I?

Dee snatched the plate up off the table. Looking at him, I smirked. What was he going to do? If he touched me, my BVP family was only a phone call away. "If you can't talk to me, you can't eat my food." He smirked back.

"I don't have to eat your damn food." I stood up; he had me messed up if he thought, I was going to ask for food I probably paid for. "My daddy probably paid for it anyway." Twisting my lips, I turned to leave.

"Your daddy ain't paid for nothing. He don't even care enough about you to call."

That hurt, but I wasn't going to let him know that. "You are a liar. You and mom spend all of our money on drugs. My daddy is a better man than you and mom still loves him." Rage burned in his eyes. That one hurt, and I knew it. I heard them arguing, so I knew my mom often said she wished she never left my dad.

"Get your ugly self out of here. You won't eat my food today or ever." Throwing the plate to the ground, he sat back down at the table. Noni got up; she wasn't going to eat either. "Sit down and finish your food girl." He told her. Noni did as she was told, but I saw the tears forming in her eyes. I gave her a look to let her know that I was okay and went to my room.

Sitting on my bed, his words burned in my brain. My dad did love me no matter what Dee said. I couldn't wait for mom to come back so I could tell her what her husband did. My anger overpowered the hunger, and I stewed until midnight came.

I was going to go find her. The house was quiet, so I knew everyone else was sleep. Creeping into Noni and my stepsister's room, I woke her up. "Shhh, we are going to go find mom. Get dressed." Noni rubbed her eyes but got up.

Tightly holding the pillowcase, I had in my hand, I walked into the kitchen. I quietly grabbed all the knives and forks and put them in it. If Dee tried to stop me, I was going to stab him. Wasn't sure what I was going to do with the forks, but I had seen enough prison movies to know that would work too.

Noni was dressed by the time I walked back into their room. My stepsister started whining; she wanted to go with us. "No, you can't come. Stay here with your daddy." I stressed *your*. Her daddy treated her right; she had no worries. She loved my mom like she was her mom, but my mom wasn't her mom. Her mom was some white woman that sent her to us because she was dark. My mom would have never done that. "She is our mom, not yours." Being the dramatic baby that she was, she put her pillow over her head like she was trying to suffocate herself.

Ignoring her, I opened the window in their room and helped Noni out. "Aren't you going to close it?" Noni asked now fully woke. "No, we got to get back in just in case we don't find mom." It was cold, and the wind was blowing hard. Good thing we put on sweaters, otherwise the trip would have been over before it started.

Mom had a friend on base that she sometimes hung out with. I knew mom got high with this lady, so that was going to be our first stop. Running, we made it the few blocks in no time. I knew it was late and all the lights were off in the house. It didn't matter; I was on a mission.

Knocking softly on the door, her dogs started barking. Pretty soon, the kitchen light came on, and the door opened. "Hey Ms. Sharon, is my mom here?" Ms. Sharon had a confused look on her face.

"Girl, what you doing out this late? No, your mama ain't here, and you need to go home." It was none of her business what I did. If my mom wasn't there, she had no purpose. Grabbing Noni hand, we left.

Sometimes mom hung out at the store by Ms. Sharon's house. We were going to head there next, but I noticed Noni was shivering. I should have left her at home. "You cold?" She nodded, so instead of heading to the store, we headed back.

When we got to the house, I saw the bedroom window was closed. I tried to open it, thinking maybe my stepsister closed it. It didn't budge. It was locked! "Damn it!" My stepsister knew how to close the window, but the lock on it was too hard for her. Dee did it. She must have gotten up when we left and told. Maybe, I should not have said that last comment. Too late now though.

Before giving up and knocking on the door, I tried all the other windows in the house. Everything was locked. The front door was the only option, so I knocked loudly. Noni had a worried look on her face. She knew I was going to get in trouble. "It's all good, don't worry." After several minutes, Dee finally opened the door. Slowly, he moved to the side and let us in. "Don't you move." He said glaring at me. Noni stopped too.

She looked up at me, and I motioned for her to go in her room. "I told you don't worry," I said, reassuring her that no matter what, I was going to be okay. She didn't need to hear what he was about to say to me. I reached for her pillowcase and hugged her before she walked off just in case. If he tried to hurt me, he was going to get stabbed.

Too many years of my life had been ruined by this man, and I was done. One of us was probably going to die or at least get seriously hurt, and I was determined that it wasn't going to be me. I stood there with no fear in my eyes with one hand on the pillowcase and the other one in it. Yep, tonight was the night. Looking up at him with all the anger I could display, I wasn't surprised to see he was frowned up too.

Not sure if this was going to be a fight or a frown off, I crossed my arms over my chest. Instead of hitting me, he cussed me out, calling me every nasty name that came to his little mind. Standing there not saying anything at all but clutching the pillowcase so tight my fingernails left prints. He saw the look in my eyes and stopped for a moment. Was that fear? I wasn't that same little girl that he manhandled and talked down too. There was no fear in my eyes. "Get out of my face." He yelled, so angrily that spit was flying out of his mouth.

It was late in the morning before mom came home. Their arguing woke me up. Footsteps were heard coming towards my room, so I sat up. It was her, I knew it. After last night, I am pretty sure Dee wasn't ready to try me just yet. Mom bust in my room without knocking. "What?" Upset from last night, I got smart right away.

"Don't you know you could have gotten killed or kidnapped? Where were you going?" She said. Anger burned in me like a hot knife and tears started forming. She was asking me where I was going, like she was gone too.

"Your husband wouldn't let me eat his food. He threw a plate, and I was trying to find you. Where were you?" Her face was blank as she rubbed her lips together. She didn't say anything, and neither did I. Eventually, the stare off was over, and she walked out slamming my door behind her.

Days passed, and nothing was mentioned about the incident, or my stuff mom took to pawn. It was summer now, and I started babysitting. I didn't like kids all that much, but I was never going to eat Dee's food if I could help it. Whenever Noni said she was hungry, we walked to the store, and I was able to buy something for her to eat. That made me feel good. We didn't need him or mom. I got us.

Not caring about anything or anyone else, if Noni was good, I was good. Dee didn't seem so big now that I could take care of myself. His day was going to come, but I wasn't sure when. Mom was lost. If it weren't for him, she would be a mom instead of someone we lived with. How could a woman stay with a man who treated her daughter like crap?

Dee didn't know where I was getting money from or how I was eating. Since I wasn't losing weight or eating his food, it bothered him. He couldn't get to me, so he started on mom. He did his best to take whatever self-esteem she had left and crush it.

He called her names and cussed her out right in front of us. When the arguments got too loud, I took Noni and my stepsister and left the house. At other times, I would holler for him to shut up.

One day, he busted into my room and asked me to repeat myself to his face. Hopping out the bed and standing up to him, we started arguing. "I said shut up." He raised his hand up. I didn't flinch. Instead, I picked up my bandanna and wrapped it around my hand. "As long as you don't touch me." He knew what that bandanna meant, and he knew what would happen if he touched me.

"You aren't worth it." He said slamming the door. Hell, maybe I should make some phone calls. Mom would be better off without him.

CHAPTER 4-NO VIEWS IN LONGVIEW

By the time I was in 8th grade, I had been back and forth between my mom and dad. Dad had a new family where he was stationed in Hawaii. I didn't fit in there either. He had his boys, finally and had changed since I had been gone. He started drinking and treated his new wife like crap. Sometimes it is better to deal with the devil you know, and I didn't know this devil my dad had become. Plus, I couldn't leave Noni alone with Dee, so I decided to just stay with mom.

Dee had gotten kicked out of the Navy, and once again, we had to move. This was the first time in my life I was going to live off base. Figuring we were moving back to Louisiana, I got happy. Dee couldn't treat us like he did if we went back there. My favorite uncle was in the military and he would not have it.

But instead, we ended up in Longview, Texas. Gang life was over for me, and we moved closer to Dee's family. Our house was ten minutes from his mother. We settled into the country town in a shack of a house. It was gray, and the paint was peeling. I knew at this point things were going to get worse. We were officially poor.

My stepsister was sent back to live with her mom since money was so tight. Dee couldn't find work, or so he said. Whatever money we did have, mom took to get high. Dee spent most of his time at his mom's house drinking all night. I was glad he was hardly home. His family didn't like my mom or us. He had told them lies, and they knew my mom was on drugs. They blamed my mom for him getting kicked out of the Navy. He was a grown man and made his own decisions. But they didn't see it that way.

They thought I was a bad seed and didn't know or care how he treated us. They didn't know how evil he was or that he broke up my family. I didn't care how they felt though. I didn't want no part of them anyway.

Unlike in Cali, school wasn't an escape; it was torture. There was no gang set to be part of. Just a bunch of wannabe kids who watched one too many gang movies. They had no idea what it was like to be jumped in or any of that.

My California accent made me stand out, and the kids made fun of me. It was a small school and Dee's niece, Torie, went there also. Torie was big, black, and ugly, like the rest of his family. She hated me and made sure everyone knew we were poor and my mom was the "crackhead" that her uncle married.

Since we were "poor," we had to get free lunch. Free lunch kids had lime green trays and a separate menu. The "paid" kids got the good food; we got the bare minimum. Yep, I was poor, and there was no hiding it. Those lime green trays could be seen from across the cafeteria. So sometimes, I ate in the library to avoid the stares and whispers. If it weren't for the fact that sometimes we didn't have food at home, I never would have eaten at school.

Between school and Dee's mom treating us like dirt, life was harder than it had been. Mom made us go to her house sometimes when she was going to be gone a few days on a binge. She talked about my mom to anyone who would listen. "She came around shaking her fast tail in front of my son. Now he is miserable. So sad how he let her bring him down to nothing. If he had listened to me, I told him, don't you date no woman with kids. Now they are always over here with these bad kids begging for food." She was on the phone talking to God only knows. She wanted us to hear her. I didn't understand how someone who was a grandmother could be so evil.

Wanting to say something, but knowing I couldn't, I sat and listened. It was bad enough we had to bring our own toilet tissue and clean the toilet with bleach if we used it, but now this. I would pee on myself before I used her bathroom. If Noni couldn't hold it, I cleaned up after her. My sister wasn't going to clean her toilet. That was probably the only time it got clean anyway.

There was a lot I couldn't control, but there were a few things I could. We were not going over there anymore. "If you make us go back over there, I am going to kill that old woman in her sleep or better yet, put bleach in her drinks," I told my mom one night. She knew I was serious; juvenile detention would be better than this life. Needless to say, we didn't have to go over there anymore.

Many nights I stayed in my room reading comics and writing in my diary. Even though we didn't have the safety of the base, I had a dog and a knife. If someone came in, me or my dog would handle it.

Besides the girl across the street, I didn't have any friends. She introduced me to her boyfriend's brother, Anthony, who I lost my virginity to in the backyard. We only talked a few times after that, but it was weird. Even though I didn't know what sex felt like, I expected to feel love. There was nothing, not even blood to indicate I had lost my virginity.

He was probably going to disappear anyway like my dad did. Better I get rid of him than the other way around, but when I went to Anthony's house the next day to break up with him, he was already gone. His parents sent him to live with family in Mississippi since he was starting to get in trouble.

Feeling shame on top of feeling abandoned, I ran home. Sitting on the bed crying, I felt that familiar friend comforting me. Hate! I hated me; I hated my life. When the girl across the street got pregnant, her mom had her on lockdown. I couldn't even talk to her. My diary was my only friend.

Spending hours in the woods behind our house, I wrote out my feelings. I hid from them and the world. Creating my own world in my diary, I wanted to go there in real life. I was numb, full of anger, and started having suicidal thoughts. Since I didn't like pain, killing myself wasn't an option. Plus, it was a sin, and going to heaven was my only solace.

After hanging out in the woods one day, I came home to find the door to my room open and my diary on my bed. Dee had gone in there and read it. "Her hot self is having sex with guys in the back of the house. You need to do something with your child." He told my mom who looked sober for once and a little disgusted.

"He should not have been in here. This is all I have that is mine." I said picking up my diary.

"Did you have sex?"

"No, mom!" I lied. "I just wrote that."

Regardless of what, I didn't want my mom to know that. If he read my diary, he also read the letter I wrote to mom. In the letter, I told her if she didn't leave him, I was going to run away and never come back. I also told her that when we were in the hotel in San Diego all those years ago, he tried to touch me. I never got a chance to give her that letter, so she never found out.

Dee didn't say anything about the letter, but he let me know he saw it. He already violated me by trying to touch me and reading my diary; there was nothing left. Except for my dog, Homey.

Homey was abandoned in the woods as a puppy, and mom let me keep him. He kept me safe and would bark at Dee when he got loud with me.

Dee had been trying to get rid of him since day one since he had fleas. I think it was really because Homey loved me and made me happy. My happiness or rather destroying what little happiness I had left was Dee's mission. He hated me, and that was okay. I hated everybody, except Noni and Homey.

One day out of the blue, he decided he was going to turn Homey into an attack dog. He started slapping him hard in the face with a black glove, and Homey was whining. Hearing him, I ran into the living room and yelled for him to stop. Homey's yelps got louder as Dee hit him harder.

"Leave my dog alone!" Suddenly, mom ran in. Since she couldn't save me, at least she could save my dog.

"Dee stop it please." She said pleading.

"Tell him to stop; he is hurting Homey." Pleading with mom, but she just looked at me helplessly defeated, between Dee and the drugs; she was gone. She didn't do anything. I guess she was scared. Then he did the unthinkable; he threw Homey against the wall.

Homey laid on the floor barely breathing and not moving. He killed Homey! Something in me clicked! I ran into the kitchen and picked up a knife out of the sink. All the years of fighting and yelling had finally driven me crazy. I started running after him with it, but mom grabbed me around my waist mid-swing.

The knife ended up in the wall a few inches from his head. His eyes got buck. All of us were in disbelief as I screamed. The knife sliced me and watching the blood go everywhere, it didn't seem real. After that, everything happened so fast. Dee broke the glass table and said I need to get the f out of his house, Homey got up and ran out of the front door. I guess he wasn't dead.

Mom wrapped a towel around my finger and tried to comfort me. Dee stormed into my room and started grabbing my clothes out of the closet. Marching through the house, I wondered what he was going to do with them. It wasn't long before I knew. He threw my clothes outside on the front porch. "She got to get out of my damn house."

It was snowing that night. It never snowed in Texas, and he was going to have to make me get out. Standing there stone-faced holding the towel around my finger, I didn't move. It hurt like hell, but I wasn't about to show it. I was angry. Why did I miss? They were arguing as mom tried to get him to let me stay. As I said, I didn't move and instead stared at the blood on the wall and my clothes. The knife was still there. Maybe I could grab it and finish what I started.

Suddenly, he grabbed me and started dragging me to the door. I was yelling, screaming and trying to swing at him. Mom tried to pull me back in, but he pushed her off him and threw me out the door onto the porch.

Mom grabbed Noni, spit in his face, and we left. We picked my clothes up and put them behind the raggedy station wagon that sat in the front yard. Mom handed me my jacket, and we started walking. I should have been cold, but my anger kept me warm, and I refused to put my jacket on.

We ended up at a motel a few miles down the road. The people hanging outside had "that" look. Hookers were trying to flag down cars, and guys were smoking weed. It was that kind of motel. Mom looked pitiful, and I knew she felt bad for having us in a place like that. But to be honest, our neighborhood wasn't that much different.

Mom didn't have any money I knew that, but somehow, we ended up in a room. Noni fell fast asleep on the bed and mom cleaned my finger. "Do you want to go get stitches?" I shook my head "no," I was more scared of needles than the pain. "You sure? If you do, they probably will ask you what happened." I didn't understand where she was going with this. "If you tell them, they would take you and your sister from me."

"No mom. It will be okay. It doesn't even hurt no more." I lied.

She got up to leave once I laid down to get settled. "I will be back," she told me leaving out of the door. It bothered me to think about what she had to do for us to get a room, but for the first time in a while, I had respect for her.

There was no turning back now. Either I was going to kill Dee, or he was going to kill me. The only difference was, I wasn't scared to die, and I am pretty sure he was. Hours later, still deep in my thoughts, mom came banging on the door. "Holy Spirit! Holy Spirit." She yelled. Holy Spirit was our code word.

"What's wrong?" I asked opening the door.

"Nothing, wake up your sister." She told us to go outside and get in the cab that was waiting. Hopping in the cab, I hoped we were going to a bus station. When the cab pulled down the familiar dark street where our little shack was, I knew different.

We were going back to the house. "I am going to kill him one day." Even though I said it low, mom heard me but didn't say anything. Pretty soon, we were back at the house and Dee was standing in the door. Noni and I stood in the driveway as mom walked up and talked to him. She was begging. I could not believe it!

He moved to the side with a disgusted look on his face and let us back in. It was then I realized that no matter what, mom wasn't going to leave him.

Dee didn't want me in his house anymore, and mom knew I was determined to end his life. Next time, she might not be there to save him. A week later, mom, Noni, and I were on a Greyhound headed back to Louisiana.

Life was changing. Things were going to be okay or, so I thought, but a week later mom and Noni headed back. She had dropped me off in Louisiana, and her choice was made. It wasn't me.

CHAPTER 5-BACK IN THE BOOT

Living with my grandmother was different. Everyone had moved out, and it was just her and me. She lived in a nice neighborhood and went to work every day. I hated the fact that I had to leave Noni, but Dee liked her, and she would be okay.

In your teenage years, you want to be accepted and fit in. I was like any other teenager; I wanted name brand clothes and all the other things that made you popular. Name brand clothes were important in Louisiana. In California, I could get away with wearing whatever, but not here. I stood out like a sore thumb. People made fun of my "valley girl" accent. To add to my low self-esteem, I became very self-conscious of the way I talked. Playing sports seemed like the thing to do, but I wasn't the best at it. It seemed like I couldn't win at home or school. Life was hard, and I hated it.

A year later, mom and Noni moved back to Louisiana. Dee came too. They moved into the house next door to my great grandmother. Mom was still on drugs. Being home with people she knew made it easier for her to find them.

Dee couldn't hang, and a year later, he left to go back to Texas. Now with him gone, I figured mom would get her act together, but she didn't. I moved back in with her and Noni. Things were worse than ever. Sometimes, we wouldn't hear from her for days at a time, and the family decided they had to do something.

For a while, Noni and I lived with my grandmother. Something in Noni had changed, she wasn't the same little sister I left. She was mean and would often tell me I couldn't tell her what to do. My grandmother couldn't handle all the fighting and sent us to live with my aunt.

Around this time, we started getting a check from the state. I didn't know what it was for, but we didn't get it anyway. Living with my grandmother wasn't so bad, but my aunt was another story.

At family get-togethers, my mom would come over to my great-grandmother's house to see us and get food. She lived in a crack house around the corner. Everyone made her feel bad an unwanted except me and Noni. "Get your cracked-out self away from here. When are you going to get your kids?"

They would try to make her leave, but my great-grandmother wasn't having it. That was still her grandchild, and if nothing else, my mom could get food and talk to us outside.

By the time I was in 10th grade, I had started dating drug dealers. They had something that I needed, money. Drug dealers always had more than one woman. I knew I was one of many, but that was okay. I got serious about one, which was a no-no.

"Is that your mom?" He asked one day picking me up. She was hanging outside at my great-grandmother's house. We looked enough alike that anyone could see we were related.

"No, let's go," I said. She looked hurt, she heard me. I felt bad after saying it, but if they knew each other, I knew why. Dating a drug dealer was one thing, dating one who sold drugs to my mom was a whole other. I left him alone.

CHAPTER 6-SAME ISH, DIFFERENT DAY

When my mom became a full-on drug addict, my sister and I were forced to live with my aunt permanently. My aunt treated us like she treated my mom. Bad. It was like we weren't even related to her. We were more like tenants and paid rent.

My older cousin, Miko, was mean to us too. She didn't like sharing her mom's time with us. I told her I wasn't looking for another mother, especially not hers. My aunt was a wannabe Christian who made us go to church and Bible study.

Before I came to live with them, my cousin and I got along. We partied and would drink together. She was not well-liked by other girls because of her cocky attitude. If she weren't my cousin, I probably would not have dealt with her either. That all changed when we moved in though.

Noni and I had to share a room, which is something we never had to do before. She wasn't the little girl that I had to protect anymore, and frankly, I had my own stuff to deal with. So, when she started cutting school, I minded my own business. If she wanted to do dumb stuff, then so be it.

Life wasn't so bad, but it was still far from good. Since no one was trying to pay for me to get my hair done, I became pretty good at doing it myself. All those years watching mom doing her makeup, I got good at that too.

It was a pretty day outside, and I had plans to go to one of my classmate's house. When the weekend hit, and even sometimes during the week, I would go by one of my friends. Anywhere, but there.

Upstairs doing my hair and makeup, I heard Miko laughing and talking. She was loud, and I figured she had company. That was something else we weren't allowed to do. Have friends over. Hearing my name, I opened the door so that I could hear better. Miko was talking loud on purpose; she wanted to make sure I heard her. "... if their mom wasn't a crackhead." It was followed by loud laughter.

For some reason, she felt like it was important for her friends to know that she didn't want us there and my sister and I were only there because my mom was "the" crackhead. I had to wear her clothes because we didn't have none; we were making their bills go up and everything. She was repeating things I know she heard from my aunt, but she still was repeating them.

I got up and walked downstairs like Ms. Sophia on *The Color Purple*. A little scared because she was bigger than me, but so was Dee and I stood up to him. My mom could not stand up for herself, and as her child, that was my job. "Why don't you shut up talking about my mom?" I said. She stood there with a slick smile on her face. She knew she had touched a nerve. Miko looked me up and down like I was dirty. "Well, it is true. Get out of my face crack baby." Her friends were silent.

Maybe they felt the tension or knew she was dead wrong. Maybe they saw the look in my eyes that I was ready to kill her. Either way, there was silence.

"Your mamas on crack rock!" She sang in my face, mocking me. Turning to go back upstairs, I felt tears well up in my eyes. She wasn't worth the trouble. It would be too easy for me to whip her.

Instead of being quiet and leaving me alone, Miko started to follow me up the stairs. "You are just like your mama, a crack ho!" That did it!

Before I could think, my body reacted, and I exploded right on top of her head, punching her as hard as I could. Pulling her hair, I drug her to the ground. She tried to fight back, but I was too quick and hit too hard. Her friends yelled for us to stop, but none of them were crazy enough to jump in. I had years of anger and hate built up; she was going to pay for everyone else.

She was bigger than me, but it was an easy win. She didn't know how to fight. She was on the ground; I was on top of her trying to kill her when my aunt came home. Hearing all the commotion and seeing me on top of her daughter, she ran up the stairs. My aunt was bigger than Miko but made it up the stairs like a track star. She screamed for me to stop and get off her daughter. But I didn't. Taking the oversized umbrella, she carried in her hand, she hit me with all her might in my back. That ended the fight.

Running into my room, I started packing a bag. I was going to leave. Not knowing or caring where I was going, I left out of the door. I didn't care if I had to stay on the street. Anything was better than this.

It was dark, and I hoped somebody came along and killed me. The only place I could think to go was my grandmother's house. She only lived a few miles away, and I could walk that. When a blue show truck slowed down beside me, I figured this was it. The window rolled down, and I saw a fat guy who reminded me of *Biggie*. "Hey, where you going? It is too dark out here for you to be walking." He said.

"I'm going up the road to my grandmother's. I'm good." Turning my head and walking faster, he still followed. "Hop in; I will give you a ride. It is too dangerous for you to be walking out here like that."

I debated on it for a minute and got in his truck. If he tried something, I could outrun him for sure. "You sure you're okay?" He asked looking concerned. I nodded my head thinking to myself he was older than I thought. Tears and snot running down my face, I guess I didn't look okay.

I pointed out where to turn to go to in my grandmother's apartments. He pulled up to the door and stopped. "Whatever it is, you are going to be alright." Thanking him, I got out his truck. He didn't know me, so what did he know? I wasn't okay and hadn't been okay since my dad left.

It was late, and my grandmother should have been asleep. I beat on the door like I was crazy. "What happened?" was the first thing she said as she opened the door. I guess my aunt called her. The look on her face wasn't one of pity. Instead, she looked like *what the hell* I was doing at her house and asked me that much.

"I'm not going back. Why can't I live here?" I asked.

Since she didn't let me past the hallway, I knew that wasn't

an option.

"No, you can't live here. You need to go back and

try to work things out." Work things out? Did she not know

what happened? Or did she not care? "Don't worry about

it; I will be good," I said grabbing her house phone by the

door.

Calling my friend, Abby was hard, but I knew I had to

call her. She knew what I was dealing with at home and

offered for me to come stay with her before. My

grandmother looked on. She loved me, but not enough to

let me live with her.

After getting the okay from Abby, I left out of the

door walking again. Abby met me at the gate of my

grandmother's apartments. She lived with her mom and

brother not far from my grandmother. This was going to be

my new home at least until I graduated.

CHAPTER 7-THE BEGINNING OF THE END

My family didn't like me living with white people. That was on them; I was finally someplace where I was treated like a person. I was part of their family. As long as I wanted to stay there, they were willing to have me.

My family wasn't having it and decided to have a "family" meeting. From outside my aunt's door, I could hear women talking. Not being able to make out their exact words, I decided to knock.

Women I recognized from my grandmother's and aunt's church sat on the couch. I stood there as they looked me up and down. "Come in and sit down," my grandmother said.

It was an ambush. And just like a timer went off, the women started talking. They were trying to get me to move back in with my aunt. Were they crazy? I wasn't listening to them, and it was obvious. So, they pulled the race card. "They really don't like colored folks and just want you to clean up behind them." One lady said. *Really, who even still said colored folks?*

"What are you talking about old lady?" I said defiantly. I was going to let them talk about Ms. B like that. They looked appalled and decided I must have had a demon in me.

When they brought out the Bible and holy water, I knew they were crazy. I didn't understand all the fuss; my aunt didn't want me there. All she wanted was the check that came with me.

As a last resort, they called my mom to come over.

Like that was going to work. I was almost 18; there was

nothing any of them could do. They were making me mad,

and I called Abby who brought me a cigarette. We talked

outside and smoked until I saw my mom pull up. Mom got

out the car kissing the old dude who was driving. I knew

what she had been doing; she wasn't dating him. Her

standards had to be higher than that, at least in the past.

Now that she was into drugs, there wasn't any telling who

she would mess with.

I didn't bother to put my cigarette out. What is a

cigarette to a crackhead? As I expected, she didn't say

anything about me smoking. She just smiled and hugged

me. I didn't want to hug her back, but I did. "What is this

all about?" She asked. Telling her what happened, I could

see the anger in her eyes.

"That is foolishness, but I hoped you whipped her butt." She said referring to the fight with my older cousin. Anytime I got in fight, that was mom's only concern, that I didn't lose. This was all her fault; why was she so angry?

She looked bad and smaller than I remembered. "They think they are better than us. They aren't. At least I am real about my life. Don't you ever back down and don't ever let anyone make you feel like you aren't nothing."

"Yes ma'am," I said looking at her. Her knees were scraped up and bruised. She had gotten drug by a car trying to buy crack a week before. "What is it going to take for you to stop? You could have died instead of been hurt. Noni and I would not have to live with other people. We could live with you." Her eyes were glazed over. She was high now, and the last thing she was thinking about was my problems.

"Look G, you are old enough to understand. You were always the strong one like your daddy. I enjoy getting high. It makes me feel good. But no matter what I have ever done, I always loved my girls. If I die, at my funeral you remember to say that. No matter what I did, I always loved my girls."

There was nothing else to be said. She liked getting high and I was strong enough to handle whatever happened because of that.

CHAPTER 8-REMORSE IN DEATH

May 25, 1994, was like any other day until I arrived home. Abby drove the long way home so that we could smoke cigarettes after school. I didn't know why she smoked, Abby had a great life. Her mom was supportive and did everything for her and her brother.

I wished my mom was more like her mom. Abby and her mom made sure whatever I needed, I had. A month earlier, she even let me borrow a prom dress from her. They were the family I wished I had.

We got out of the car and walked into her mom's office to check in. Usually bright and smiling, Ms. B looked like she had seen a ghost. "Your grandmother is on her way to get you," she said.

I sighed. My heart got heavy. "What's wrong?" I asked Ms. B, who didn't say anything. Abby and I looked at each other and shrugged. Something inside of me hurt, and I needed to know why she was coming to get me. "Is my sister pregnant? I asked.

"No just wait until your grandmother gets here."

"What? Is my momma dead?" What made me say that and why she wasn't she telling me? But, the look on her face told me everything I needed to know.

How could she be dead? Somebody was lying. Maybe this was another plot to get me to go back to my aunt's house for a white people intervention. When the air was sucked out of me, I knew it was true. I didn't know what to say next; I was in shock. Why did I always have to be right? Was I in a bad dream that just seemed real? How did I even know?

Never did I imagine my mom not being there. I figured she would get her life together in time for me to graduate high school. What about when I got married and had kids? Who was going to be their grandmother? She could not be dead.

I felt an overwhelming sensation of guilt. I had put her on the backburner, and now the backburner had burned out. I fell to my knees, not having the strength to cry or stand any longer. Tears started rolling down my cheeks as thoughts flashed through my mind. Just three weeks before, she told me what to say at her funeral. Did she know she was going to die? Did she kill herself? How could this even be real? Who loses their mother at 17?

A horn blowing outside brought me back to the present moment. It was my great-grandmother's neighbor and old family friend. Abby hugged me; she had been crying. I still wasn't ready to accept it as being true. I went outside and got in his car anyway. He didn't say anything to me, and I didn't say anything to him. Maybe my mom was just seriously hurt. She couldn't be dead. Death was final.

Feeling sad, guilty, and enraged at the same time, I almost jumped out of his car. He was driving ten miles below the speed limit, and I didn't even know where we were going.

When we pulled up to my great-grandmother's house, I saw all the cars lined up. Whatever it was, it was serious. The windows of the car were rolled up, but I could still hear Noni. My baby sister was screaming like someone was hurting her. Jumping out of the car and running towards the house, I was ready for whatever came my way. If they were trying to hurt my sister or my mom, I was going to kill everyone.

Noni came out running towards me screaming. She fell into my arms crying and yelling. "They are lying! Mom's not dead!" Her eyes were almost swollen shut and were wet with tears. "They're lyin! Mom's not dead!" She screamed again. Seeing my sister losing her mind made me break down. My body started shaking, and I thought I was going to die too. I wanted to die. At that moment, I couldn't be strong anymore.

It had been a hard, horrible life for my mom. I didn't make it any better. Ignoring her and even denying her. I was a terrible daughter. She would never know how much I loved her. Now it was too late to right my wrongs. For the first time, my anger turned to shame and guilt.

My grandmother came outside and pulled us into the house. She wanted our grief to be private, but Noni was making a scene. Why did they even tell Noni without me being there?

Watching them made me feel disgusted; they were acting like they cared about what happened to my mom. They didn't have the right to cry or feel hurt. If they really loved my mom, they would have forced her to get better. Instead, they let the problem go on and on. Just like it was too late for me, it was too late for them. She was gone.

Feelings of anger rose back up in me. No one cared about my mom except my sister and me. They weren't going to see me cry. They weren't going to see her daughter be weak. I fought off the tears as best as I could. That worked until the news came on. "A body found in a ditch in Zachary with two gunshot wounds to the head has been identified as Griezelda Jones of Baton Rouge. There are no suspects." It is said she lived a "high-risk lifestyle..."

I didn't hear anything after that. They didn't have the right to demean her on TV. I didn't care how her lifestyle was, that was my mom, and she was dead. In a ditch? Who killed her? Did they know she was someone's mom? Did she look at our pictures when she knew she was going to die?

Everyone started acting crazier... crying, screaming, slobbering. I felt lost. I would never see my mom's beautiful face again or hear her laugh. Nothing mattered! Noni and I sat in the corner huddled together like five-year-olds. Everyone tried to comfort us. Now!

My mom's brother told me to calm down and be strong. I looked at him. This coming from the family pervert. Rolling my eyes, I held Noni tighter. No mom, no dad...we were orphans. "Hold it together; you have to be strong for your sister." My mom was dead at only 34 years old, and I could not cry because I had to be strong for Noni.

"It will be okay. I promise." I lied, nothing would never be okay again.

Still trying to comfort us, they started telling us things that didn't make sense like; she is in a better place. How could she be in a better place? Any place where we weren't together wasn't better. They could all go to hell. I wanted my mommy, and that was all.

CHAPTER 9-THE FUNERAL

At Abby's house, I was able to get away from the family's pretense and fake tears, so I stayed there. Days later, I was still numb and didn't want to talk or be around anybody.

A day before the funeral, I got an unexpected phone call. "Valencia, it's your dad," Abby said reaching me the phone. It had been over five years since I had last talked to him. I thought she was joking, surely somebody was.

He disappeared, and I didn't understand why he stopped calling us, but I guess that is what happens when you have a new family. How did he even know to call or where I was? Did he know about mom?

"Hello," I said listening for the person on the other line to fess up. "G," he said low. No matter how much time had passed, I recognized his voice. "Dad, daddy. Where are you? Where have you been? Mom..."

He cut me off. "I know. We will talk about that later. I just need you to go back home, go back to your grandmother's house."

"No, I can't! I can't stay there."

"Listen, you have to. You won't have to stay there long. I'm sorry about what happened to your mom. I will come and get you and your sister." He said the magic words.

"Promise?"

"Promise," he said.

We got off the phone, and I felt everything was going to be alright. He was coming to get us. My dad was coming to save the day. Being an obedient daughter, I moved back to my grandmother's house that day.

Going back to my grandmother's put me back in the middle of the madness. I laid in my bed listening to them discuss my mom's funeral like it was an event. They were discussing colors and what everyone should wear. Who color coordinates a funeral? And still, no one asked if I was okay. I became an expert in acting like nothing bothered me. Not the ugly names I was called, not my mom's drug problem, not even her death. I became numb to everything.

At the funeral, I saw people who I hadn't seen in years. All the people who had abandoned my mom in her time of need suddenly appeared. The crowd was big, but I didn't see my dad. My sister was crying, but I didn't.

Lined up in the front of the funeral home there were so many preachers. My grandmother, no doubt, set that up. My mom didn't go to church. Where were the preachers when she was living in the crack house? Nowhere to be found, but they were here now dressed in full armor getting ready to tell stories about someone they didn't know.

All the family sat together putting on a good unified front for the onlookers. We were all dressed in white. No wonder my mom was messed up. It was a funeral, and it looked like a damn fashion show. I looked at them with contempt. Anyone of them deserved to be there, not my mom lying in a casket.

Both my aunt and Miko were putting on a show falling out and crying loudly. Miko stood in the hallway crying and breaking down. She drew so much attention that the "church ladies" went over there waving fans to calm her down. I wanted to holler at them to shut up. Other people probably thought they were really hurt, but I knew the truth.

I rolled my eyes in disgust and focused on the casket. The whole funeral home looked shabby. My mom's bloated body laid in the cheap brown casket. Her face was swollen. It wasn't swollen when I saw her a few weeks ago.

The preachers took turns getting up for their five minutes of fame. The whole funeral was longer than I thought it should have been. The show from the preachers took a lot of time. They strained their voices trying to outdo each other. Finally, they were done. I had to stand up for my mom and say what she asked me to.

Walking up to the podium was scary, and I felt weak. There was dead silence in the room as everyone looked at me. I was hot, sweaty and pretty sure I was going to pass out right there in front of everybody. Standing up there, I held on to the podium for dear life. The room looked bigger from up there. I looked down at the paper; the words were squiggly. My hands were shaking when I wrote it, and the water in my eyes didn't help.

As the oldest and the only one in the room who knew my mom, I had to do it. I opened my mouth, but nothing came out. My throat felt dry. I prayed, *Lord, help me find my voice.* Swallowing hard, I tried again.

"For those who don't know me, I am Griezelda's oldest daughter. My mom told me what to say at her funeral three weeks ago. Neither one of us knew it was going to be the last time we talked. It was like she knew she was going to die. She wanted me to say that no matter what..." my voice started breaking off. I stopped, and a tear fell. "She never asked me for anything, so I owe her this much. No matter what she did, she loved us. She lived and died loving her girls." Tears started falling. "She…" I couldn't fight it anymore. I broke and started shaking my head indicating I was done. Somebody came and escorted me back to my seat.

On the way down, I looked in the casket again. I had to know if it was really her. Maybe, Noni was right. Maybe it was all some plot. The lady in the casket had on light makeup, and her hair wasn't combed right. Anyone who knew my mom knew she wore dark makeup and her hair was always combed a certain way. The dress she had on was ugly and old-fashioned. Noni and I were her only children. Why did no one ask us about her hair, makeup or outfit?

The funeral was done, and it was time for the viewing. As everyone passed, they touched me and my sister's hand. They walked up slowly looking in the casket saying soft words to my mom's body. I could tell they were surprised how she looked. They told us how sorry they were and that my mom was a good person. The fakeness was overwhelming.

Friends, family, then Noni and I would go. When my aunt went up there, she looked at my mom's body and let out a scream. "Not my sister!" She fell out right there in front of the casket. First, it was her, then her daughter, then the rest of my family. It was like a chain reaction. Everyone was falling out, except my sister and me.

Suddenly, the funeral director closed the casket. I sat there stunned. Were they going to open it back up? How were they going to close it without my sister and I saying goodbye? It was our mom dammit! But they didn't open it back, and we were rushed off to the burial place. That was it! We didn't get to say goodbye.

The limo pulled up to the spot where my mom was to be buried in the middle of nowhere at an unkept graveyard. It looked as if it had never been tended to, ever. I wish I were older; I wish I had money. I would have made sure she was buried in a decent place.

There was just a hole, no headstone, no flowers... nothing. They lowered her in the ground. "Why are y'all burying her here?" I managed to ask my grandmother.

"That was all we could afford," she said like I didn't have the right to ask. As they lowered mom into the ground, Noni was trying to get in the hole. It took three people to hold her back. And just like that, it was over! We never had the chance to say goodbye.

CHAPTER 10-READY TO DIE

Moving back in with my grandmother at my father's suggestions was a mistake. He never showed up. Things with my grandmother had changed. Even though I lost my mom, she lost a child, and I knew she hurt too. She didn't fuss as much when I went out to get drunk. Instead, she prayed for me and left it alone.

I was on a one-woman path to destroy myself and really didn't care if death came for me. Mom's murder was still unsolved, and it didn't seem like no one was trying to find out what happened. I wanted to join her. It was too much. No one cared or was affected like my sister and me, and they went on with life as usual. She was just someone living a "high risk" life... just another drug user.

Going on autopilot, I graduated high school a year later. After graduation, I partied harder. There was no direction, no plan, nothing. No one put up money from our checks, so I didn't even have money. Why not waste away?

Even though Miko wasn't my favorite person, we hit the clubs together. This was going to one of those nights where I knew something was going to go down. Still feeling the pain of mom's death and her not seeing me graduate, I had it on my mind. Tonight, I was going to let some of this anger out.

This time though, it wasn't me, it was Miko. Miko got into it with some girls flirting with the guy she dated. I stood in the corner smoking a cigarette and just watched them on the dancefloor. The other girls were trying to start mess, dancing close to Miko and our play cousin, Iesha.

When one of the girls bumped into me hard; I turned around. I shook my finger at her. "I'm not the one." I mouthed. When she bounced closer to my face, I hit her.

Her friends tried to jump me, but Miko and Iesha started swinging. Security moved in quick and put us all out the club. They were still yelling and talking crazy. I flipped them off with one hand and flipped my BVP sign with the other. I wasn't a regular chick. Even though it had been years since I left the gang, it was still in me. Plus, my mom just died; I was dangerous to everyone, including myself.

When we made it to the car, the guy Miko was dating was standing next to it. After talking with him, she got in the car and screeched out of the parking lot.

Running every red light between the club and my grandmother's house, I don't know how we made it. But when I looked up, we were there. I threw my deuces up and got out the car.

Holding onto the rail, I barely made it up the concrete stairs. I had fallen on them many times before coming home drunk and those stairs hurt. With my clothes still on, I passed out on the bed.

In a deep coma type sleep, I thought I was dreaming when I heard a knock at the window. I looked at the clock; it was 4 am. Who the hell was that? I pulled the curtain back and saw Iesha standing there looking nervous. Something was wrong.

"Miko is over at DQ's house, and her drunk self is about to get jumped. The girls we fought at the club over there." I was confused, half sleep and not understanding nothing she was saying.

"What?" I asked rubbing my eyes. "Miko is about to get jumped!" That woke me all the way up. "And you left her?" I rolled my eyes grabbing my tennis shoes. She was scared but being that she woke me up from a drunk sleep I didn't care if I hurt her feelings.

"Somebody is going to get whipped for this. I can't believe you left her over there." Iesha drove fast to get over to DQ's house. Both of us were worried about Miko. She couldn't fight sober, much less drunk.

As soon as we pulled up in his parking lot, I hopped out of the car. I ran up to the front door and banged on it like I was the police. DQ opened it up. "Bruh, get your cousin." He said with slurred speech. He was drunk, and I could smell the brown liquor on his breath. I looked at him and everybody else sitting in the living room getting high.

Miko was sitting on his bed like a little kid with her arms across her chest. The girls from the club were talking crazy. It was more of them, and we were outnumbered three to one. I was all the way sober then. "Look, girl, let's go," I said pulling her arm. She was swaying from side to side as I pulled her off his bed. We made it to the living room then she fell on the couch. We had to get out of there.

Trying to pull Miko up and looking for help, I noticed Iesha had disappeared. Just then, one of the girls pushed Miko off the couch. "Back up!" I yelled. Outnumbered or not, I wasn't going to let my cousin get pushed around. Miko laid on the floor not trying to get up. Before I could do anything else, my aunt bust in the door with Iesha behind her.

DQ went up to her trying to explain how this wasn't his fault. My aunt ignored him and instead started yelling at my cousin. "Miko get up!" She yelled pulling her arm.

Miko told her "no," and sat back down on the floor. For some reason, she wasn't comprehending the situation. There were at least six girls in there ready to fight her. Plus, she looked real stupid.

My aunt started popping her on her leg. It was kind of funny. Miko, embarrassed because the girls were laughing at her, finally started to get up off the floor.

"Yeah, go with your moms. He doesn't want you anyway." Miko started talking crazy on the other side of my aunt. She got real brave then. One of the girls had a cordless phone in her hand and swung it at her. I was watching the whole thing. Even though I didn't like my aunt or Miko really, I wasn't going to let them get hit. Swinging like a prizefighter, I punched the girl in the face. I kept hitting her as hard as I could. It happened so fast, and I was hitting so hard, no one jumped in.

When I looked up to see if Iesha, Miko, or my aunt was fighting, they were gone. Leaving me in there to fend for myself. This wasn't even my fight. I grabbed the girl's hair and dragged her outside. There was no way I was going to get jumped. Once we got outside, I started to hit her again, but then I heard a firecracker!

It wasn't fourth of July, so I knew what that noise was. The girl's friend had gone to their car and got a gun. Letting the girl's hair go, I started to run. Everyone was in the car by that time, except me, so my aunt started to pull off. I didn't think my aunt was dirty enough to leave me there, but I didn't put anything past her. This is the same woman who beat me with an umbrella years ago.

The girl handed her friend the gun and started running towards us shooting. I stopped running as she got close to me. *"F that!"* I was tired and drunk. Most of all I was ready to die and if it was my time, so be it.

Turning around to face my death, I smirked. "If you shoot me, it is going to have to be in my face." She pointed it at my chest, and I felt the cold weight of the gun against me. I didn't flinch. "Shoot me! But you better kill me!" Maybe this was how my life was supposed to end. I expected to die by a gun; I just thought it would be my own mess.

The girl's eyes got big; maybe she never shot anyone before, maybe she was scared. Either way, she started backing up from me. Her friend grabbed her shirt and they headed back to the apartment cussing us out the whole way. I just laughed at them. Cowards! We got in the car and left like nothing happened. As we drove, I realized two things: one I had to leave Louisiana, and two, my aunt and cousin were garbage who only cared about themselves.

CHAPTER 11-FINDING LIFE

My grandmother found out what happened that night and told me I had to move out. I was not bringing that kind of drama to her house. Even though it wasn't my drama, I didn't argue. I needed to leave Louisiana anyway.

My stepmom lived in Georgia with my baby brothers. Since Noni was doing her own thing and had a baby, we weren't close anymore. There was no reason for me to stay in Louisiana. So, I packed up my stuff and hopped a Greyhound bus.

Georgia was big, and it was new. No one knew me or my past, and I could start fresh. It wasn't long before I got a job, so I had money now. Things were going pretty good, and I was able to get to know my brothers. I used to resent them for taking my dad, but they looked just like Noni and me when we were little, so eventually, I started to love them.

One day I was outside playing volleyball, and a guy in a red jeep pulled up. He asked for my number. Mel was older than me; I could tell by the way he talked. He said he was 26 and even though I was 19, he liked me. Pretty soon, we were hanging out every day when I got off work.

Even though weed made me freak out, I still tried to smoke it before I went to his house. I really liked him and hoped we would get serious. He wasn't looking for a relationship though, just the benefits of one. He got more than what he bargained for. Two months later, I was pregnant.

The two blue lines didn't lie and neither did the doctor. Funny thing is, I knew I was pregnant from the moment it happened. My body felt different, and for the first time in a long time, I didn't want to die. I had a life growing inside of me. Somebody I was going to be responsible for.

Even before the doctors told me the gender, I knew it was going to be a boy. He was going to be raised right. Having my son almost three years after my mom's death was a wakeup call. More like a blaring alarm when you are in a drunk sleep.

It was far from planned, but there I was about to be a parent. No longer did I have the option of not being here. Even though I didn't know how to parent, I was going to be the best at it. It is hard to know how to do something you never experienced or seen before. My plan was just to do the opposite of everything I ever saw.

Mel and I talked, he wasn't ready to be a father. He had a choice, but I didn't. Georgia was so expensive. I made too much to get any assistance, but too little to provide a good life for him, so I moved back to Louisiana.

Being a parent became my only reason to live. He taught me how to love, which was something I never thought I could do. I didn't know you could love one thing so much. It also made me think about my mom a lot and wonder how my mom could choose what she did. Didn't she love Noni and I as much as I loved this baby?

For years, that question ate me up, and soon mom became just someone who gave birth to two dysfunctional girls. She was a crackhead who decided to be that. Just another murder, a statistic, a nobody. Even though, I didn't deny her existence. I let the bad memories overshadow the good to where there was no good left.

Chapter 12-Trying To Find Love

Regardless of what mom tried to speak into me before she died, there was so much I didn't know. My life had been one lie after the other, one bad choice after the other. I felt handicap trying to raise a son while trying to raise myself. I hated her for handicapping me; I hated me for being handicap; I hated everyone except my son.

I wanted him to have a picture-perfect life with a white picket fence. Things just seemed not to go that way. My quest to have a dad for him led me into a relationship that I should not have been in. One that almost destroyed me.

For years, I had dated a married guy who provided the extra I needed to care for my son. Being the typical "other" woman, I wanted more. I wanted what his wife had. He wasn't willing to give me that and felt since he paid bills and came whenever I called, that was enough. It wasn't.

Working at the newspaper, I made some money, but not enough, so his "extra" mattered. But there were nights I got lonely. Nights when he was at home with his wife that I needed him to be there with me. But he wasn't, so I filled the space. Met a guy and married him.

From the meeting to marriage was all of six months, but he seemed nice enough. He was from New Orleans, and I liked the way he talked. That was about it. Something was hidden about him. He had secrets. I knew that but didn't expect much from someone who went from a halfway house to my house.

He had a job, paid bills, and seemed to love me. But everything was not what it seemed. Before the ink was dry on the marriage license, he hit me. I had never been hit before, at least not in a relationship. So, I hit him back, and we fought.

When Jerry was sober, it was all good. Lovey-dovey family man, but when he got drunk, Jerry became the devil. Every three weeks like clockwork, we would fight. Or rather, he would beat me. It took a while for me to look at it like that, but that is what it was.

My two-year-old son knew how to dial 911, and he did. The police would come and sometimes take him to jail. Other times, they wouldn't. Jerry was so nice. When he would beg me to get him out of jail or drop the charges, I always did, until the last fight.

He came home from work drunker than usual.

"Where have you been?" I asked him, not really caring, but it seemed like the right question to ask. "None of your business and here is the money for the bills." He said throwing $50 at me.

"What am I supposed to do with this?" Our bills were way more than that, and even though I made more money, he was still my husband.

"You handle the rest. You got it money-maker and what you got on looking like a stripper." I shook my head in disgust at him. That pissed him off, and he punched me in the face.

It caught me so off guard; I couldn't react quick enough. His hands were around my neck, and my son was hollering. I didn't want my son to watch me die, so I started to fight back. Somehow, I got away from him and grabbed the knife out of my purse.

My weave was on the floor, I felt a knot on my head, and my son was on the stairs crying. Nope, Valencia, it was not going down like this. Putting the knife to his throat, I was done. I was going to kill him. But before I could do anything else, the police were at the door.

They were familiar with my address and with him. So even though I had a knife, they took him to jail. I grabbed my son, our stuff and moved in with Noni.

Many months and restraining orders later, I met someone else. I was trying to heal, but I needed love or at least something close to it. He was like a knight in shining armor. He knew what I was dealing with and moved us away from Baton Rouge. But there was one problem. Well, actually two. My ex left me with PTSD, but more importantly, my new love wasn't black.

My family had always had what I call an "all black" everything attitude. I knew it wasn't going to go over well, but I didn't care.

We were six months in, and it was time I stopped hiding. It isn't like they had ever supported me anyway. "He just wants you to be his maid." That was how they felt and said so.

Apparently, my being happy didn't matter because, at the end of the day, I was breaking the rules. I was trying to bring a "white boy" home.

Everyone had an opinion and cared about my life now. They didn't care that the abuse I suffered at the hands of my ex traumatized me. I had never been in an abusive relationship before. Yeah, I had seen people go through it, but never had someone I dated put their hands on me. Most relationships left a residue, the residue from that one was PTSD, I had developed a deep fear of black men.

At the very sight of a dark-skinned man, I would have a panic attack. It didn't make sense, and of course, I didn't seek help, not even when the nightmares started. I just knew me dating someone black was not at option anymore.

It wasn't normal, I knew that, and I wasn't supposed to fear anything but God. I had to get it together, my son is 100% black, and I didn't know how I could explain that to him.

"How are you going to raise a black man with a white man?" Someone asked.

My response was, "As long as he is raised to be a man, that is all I care about." Plenty of single black mothers have accomplished this with no man in sight.

My favorite uncle even became short with me. Some people's opinions didn't matter, his kind of did. He never said it, but the look on his face was sheer disappointment, and it hurt me.

Since my ex was stalking me, it made sense for me to move away. Moving to the next parish, I thought everything would be okay or at least better. It wasn't, and it was naïve for me to think that.

The relationship got serious; I think the opposition had a lot to do with that. Things were good for a while, but there were other issues in the relationship. In between these relationships, I hadn't dealt with my real issue. Me.

Ken had financial control and often threatened not to pay bills if I didn't act right. He became possessive, which I was not going through again. So, I cheated.

It made sense. I didn't want to leave because we had the outside life I wanted to give my son. Me being happy wasn't a big deal. Bouncing from a bad childhood to motherhood to an abusive relationship to a possessive one. I was tired of life, and it showed.

I was unhappy, unhealthy, and had migraines that would cripple me for hours. One day, it almost came to an end. I wanted it to end.

Even though it had only been an hour, my head was pounding so bad I took another pill. Ken had ripped out everything under the hood of the car, so I couldn't leave the house while he was at work. He found a number and figured I had been cheating.

My eyes started closing, they were real heavy now, and I started feeling dizzy. *"Well Valencia, maybe next life would be better. This is the end."* I said to myself. That thought comforted me; I was ready to die and had been for a long time.

Crying myself into a migraine this time, I was done. Here I was in the garage, writing, crying and dying at the same time. My head filled with thoughts of my uncle, who had committed suicide a year before. My mom, the way I grew up all the things I tried to bury, were in the forefront of my mind.

But then, there were thoughts of my son. *Maybe he would be better off without me.* He was only nine, and that would leave a whole lot of his life without me. He would probably blame himself or go into some destructive spiral like I did when my mom died. I couldn't do that to him, but now it was too late.

If I was going to die this night, I didn't want my son to find my body in the garage. I didn't want him to read the words in my diary about how much I hated myself. He didn't deserve that.

Laying there in my thoughts, counting my last breaths and wondering how long it took to die. *Would my death be ruled a suicide?* I didn't want him to think I did this on purpose, even though I kind of did.

I was a fighter, but here I was, 29 years old about to leave it all behind. Happy, sad, scared, mad. Too many emotions all at one time. I didn't love me! In fact, I hated me. This was all my fault. *Why wasn't I stronger? Was I weak like my mom? She was on drugs, and I was purposely overdosing myself. Ironic.*

My mom died, I wouldn't allow myself to break. I was molested, I didn't allow myself to break. I was abused, I didn't allow myself to break. I couldn't break now!

All I had was my son, and all my son had was me. If I didn't love me enough to stay and fight, that was okay. It wasn't okay for me to leave him. I hadn't really prayed since I was a little girl begging for food, but maybe God would listen to me one more time, it didn't hurt to try.

"Lord, I can't leave him. If I wake up, I promise everything is going to change. Everything." That was the last words I said as I passed out.

A few hours later, I woke up. Even though it was the same day, it was a new day. I had a life to start living and a promise I had to keep.

Not knowing where to start changing my life, I started simple, I had years of mental damage to undo. That is when the real work began. The first thing I had to do was start speaking life to myself. That wasn't easy; I felt like I was lying. My whole life was one of struggle and unhappiness.

My stepdad, the guys I dated, my family, and other people had all used me as a dumping ground for their negativity. And I had allowed it! I allowed myself to be buried mentally, and I was physically doing it to myself now.

Somewhere, buried under it, was the real me and I had to get to her. So, I started walking by myself and talking to myself. As I walked, I told myself how great I was. The voice of my stepdad would play in my head, but instead of feeling down, I got mad. My anger fueled my steps. My anger fueled my weight loss. My anger fueled my confidence. How dare he or anyone else tell me who I am? My neighbors would see me walking and thought I was crazy. When those negative voices came, I talked back to them. "Shut up!" I yelled at the top of my lungs.

I was losing weight and my relationship. Ken became insecure. I had to leave him, no doubt about that part. What do you do when your marriage is crumbling? I got a job and left him. It wasn't hard. Walking away became an easy pattern for me. People had walked away and disappointed me my whole life and now I could do it too.

I knew how to survive, but to raise my son right, I had to learn how to live. Somebody had to break this unhealthy cycle; it had to be me. But I had work to do.

CHAPTER 13-FORGIVING MOM

As I started to work on me, I knew had to deal with the "mom" issues. This caused me to delve into who she was, not what she became. I went to her rehab journals, that was my start. On a brief stint in rehab, she had journaled about her life. Even though I had read them before, I read them again with different eyes.

I cried as I read about her being mentally and physically abused by those she trusted. Her childhood was spent wanting to be accepted by a family who made her feel like an outsider. Just like me. There were things said and done to her that no one, not even me with my strong self, could come out of unscathed. Her pain was never addressed, and her issues never discussed. That same nobody loved me feeling that I had, she did too.

The difference between how she handled the abuse and how I did, was circumstance. I was lost like she was, but there was no comfort in drugs for me. It wasn't lack of trying to get high. Feeling like something else controlled me went against my nature. Drug career over!

Forgiving her so I could be better wasn't easy, but I had to do it for my sake and for my sons. I didn't want him thinking that his grandmother was some horrible person and "just" a drug addict.

Before drugs took over, my mom was a writer and even had poems published. She was a caring person and made dresses for Noni and me, so she could dress us alike. She made sure she was put together when she stepped out even when she was only going out to get high. She taught us how to sew our own dolls clothes so that they would have one-of-a-kind designs. She made us watch movies that scared us, so we could recognize danger when we saw it. Right or wrong, she supported my decisions and never looked down on me. There were so many more memories that I filled my head with.

These memories helped me look at her like she was a person long before she became a mom. I don't know how I would have handled being a young mother of two with a husband working all the time. I was barely handling one child. I was 20 when I became a mother; she was 17. But she did the best with what she had and who she was. At the end of the day, that is what I did too.

That summed her up. She wanted and needed love because she didn't know how to love herself. Her life had never been about *her* needs and *her* wants. Drugs had been the only thing she ever did for her.

It could have been me. That realization of how close I was to be a repeat of my mom's bad habits, helped me forgive her. It also did something else to me. It empowered me to start to love me!

It was like a lightbulb went off. I wasn't a mistake because I made some. My very DNA was strong, stubborn, and creative. The ability I had to stand on my own and do my own thing was fostered by her. I was her child, her dream, her G baby.

No matter what, I was going to be great. She somehow knew that. So, she taught me how to walk like I owned the world. She told me that anyone would be lucky to have me. Even though those lessons were buried for years in anger, when they came back to me, I knew what I had to do.

My work was just beginning; however, the forgiveness allowed me to start flourishing. There is something that happens when you start to let things go; you start to grow.

But not only did I have to forgive her, but I also had to forgive me. That was harder to accept. The guilt I carried of not being able to stop her was eating me up too. I should have been able to stop her from doing drugs, right? Wrong! There was nothing I could have done to stop her.

No matter how powerful I thought I was, I wasn't powerful enough to change her, and that was okay. There was no way for me to go back and not say things I said to her. I had to accept that it was too late to go back and do anything.

No longer was I going to be defined as the daughter of a drug addict. I was a woman who was born to take the dreams of her mother and use them as a foundation to build

something great. At least that is what I started to tell myself

and eventually, it stuck.

Epilogue

Just like that, it happened! I was settled in life and content with being single. My son and I had repaired our relationship that was broken when I left my ex. He only had a few more years left in school, and then, I would be free.

"Those who wander are not always lost" is what the caption on the dating profile said. At this point in my life, I didn't want a relationship, just company so I did a dating profile. I looked at the pictures, he had kids, and one was obviously mixed. He was attractive and looked like he would be fun.

I was ready to delete the app and just not even date. But there was something about him, so I bit the bullet and responded, "Some of them are lost," and it was a done deal.

I wasn't sure if he would respond back. My response was weird, plus I didn't even have a picture up just words on my profile. Even though I was not looking for anything serious, I wanted someone who wanted to get to know me not just respond because of what I looked like.

He responded! The first night, we talked for hours while he was working. We talked for a while before I sent him a picture of me. He was different. He was open, but he had been hurt and wasn't looking to get serious either. We were in one accord with that. Fun, exclusive, but not seriously committed.

When we finally decided to meet in person, I discovered he lived five minutes from me. We got to know each other and months later decided we were going to be committed. When his job sent him out of state to work, it became unbearable for us not to see each other. Was this love? If it was, I apparently never had felt it before. Since he was only a few hours away, I figured I could go and start visiting him on the weekends, so that meant I had to tell my son.

By this time, my son was in 10th grade and close to my ex. I didn't want to bring anyone else into his life he wasn't ready for. So, I gave him the option of deciding when he wanted to meet him. There was no weirdness, just my son sizing him up as a son would do.

Life has a funny way of directing you the way you are supposed to go. It was hard to believe that after years of knowing nothing but pain, I finally was happy and knew exactly what love was like. Love was a lifelong search for my mother and almost for me too. Years later, we went to the justice of the peace and got married. My husband was the prayer I didn't know I prayed and the person who helped heal my heart. All I ever wanted was a family that was whole.

That search led me into joining the gang and bad relationships, but I don't regret any of it.

The most important lesson I learned through all of this is you can't choose how you grow up. You can't choose your parents. You can't even choose some of the things that will make you bitter in life. However, you can choose to learn how to survive, forgive, live, and then love. It is a journey, not for the weak, but if you have hit rock bottom, you already have a foundation. Somebody must be here to tell the story because somebody is going through it.

The Writings of

GRIEZELDA L. JONES

6/23/59-5/24/94

The Author, Valencia Griffin-Wallace and
Her Mother, Griezelda Jones In 1978

"A ROSE"

Just like a rose
Our love bloomed so beautifully
We were very careful
Because we knew
Just like a rose, love is fragile

Just like a rose
Our love withered and died
Just like the petals of a rose
That fall off when it dies
The tears of heart break
Fell from my eyes

Just like a rose
That you wrap and put away
I put out love
In a corner of my heart

Just like another rose
That blooms so beautifully
One day another love
Will find its way to me

-Griezelda L. May 8, 1984

"PAPA"

Papa said don't quit school
That's what they want you to do
Study hard, hold your head high
And never swallow your pride

Papa said don't fail
That's what they want you to do
You can't fail if you keep trying
It takes plenty prayers and plenty crying

Papa said don't hurt your sister or brother
That's what they want you to do
Give respect where respect is due
And one-day people will respect you

Papa said don't quit your job
That's what they want you to do
Keep reaching, keep wanting to know
The more you want, they higher you'll go

Papa said before he died
Never toss your dreams aside
That's what they want you to do

-Griezelda L. Feb 1984

"YOU"

The first time I saw you
I knew I would love you
After the first kiss
I knew I was hooked

The first time your brown skin met mine
I knew I'd always want you
When you said you loved me?
I knew you would make me happy

The first time you left me
I didn't know what to do
When you came back
I knew I would never let you go

-Griezelda L. May 1984

"LORD"

Lord sometimes
I don't understand
How you could give your son to man

I know it hurt to see your son die
To see him suffer on the cross
It could never be easy to give your life
So, others wouldn't be lost

In this world full of lust and hate
No one seems to want to enter those gates
I'm not perfect, I still sin
But I'm determined to make it in

I know you will always be by my side
Being my friend and my guide
And when I have no one on earth to turn to
Lord I know, I'll always have you

-Griezelda L. Feb, 1984

"UNTITLED"

You destroyed my life
And broke my heart
So, I left you

I destroyed your life
And broke your heart
We both payed

Time passed
Our hearts mended
I came back

Many promises were made
Some we will keep
Some we won't

When I'm angry
I want to hurt you
But I can't

All I want is some hugs, kisses
And reassurance
But you won't give any
You're still bitter

But I can deal with it
Because living with your bitterness
Is a hell of a lot easier
Than living without you

-Griezelda L. Feb 1984

"UNTITLED"

You came in my life
At a very troubled time
You made me happy

Whenever I'm with you
I feel like I'm on a cloud
Drifting, drifting, falling in love

Not thinking, not caring
About the future, just now
Both of us forgetting
We belong to someone else

-Griezelda L. Apr 1984

"CHILDREN"

The children of this world
Are in their generation wiser
Than the children of light

The children of this world
Are born full of love and joy
Ready to learn, ready to win, ready to fight

The children of this world
Are a heritage of God, parents and the world
Rather he be red, yellow, black or white
Rather boy or girl

The children of this world
Watch them and you will see
Their smiles can melt
The coldest hearts
And their hugs can generate electricity

-Griezelda L. Mar 1984

"UNTITLED"

You can't take or make a break
Someone has to give you one

When you get one
You can make more breaks

You can't make someone love you
They have to give it freely

When they give love
You can make it grow

-Griezelda L. Mar 1984

"NOW"

Now that you've learned to send flowers
Remember birthdays and Valentine's day,
You can go do it all
For some other woman

Now that you can take someone out to dinner
And choose a bottle of wine,
Now that you know the best ways to make love to me,
Now that you've developed a sense of what I like,
You can go give it away to someone who won't need to ask

Now that you're no longer broke
Now that you have a functional car,
Now that were no longer struggling
Now that we've started a family
You want to be free to make someone else happy

Now that I've learned to meet your needs
We both have to learn
To meet the needs of someone else

It's always better when you don't have to ask
But when is someone going to come along
Who needs hardly any instruction
Someone who's already had training with someone else

-Griezelda L. May 1984

"I KNOW I CAN HURT YOU"

I know I can hurt you
But I wont
Because I love you

I won't be jealous
Of an old girlfriend or ex-wife
I can only envy something
I dreamed for myself

She isn't me and I'm not her
That's why I'm here and she isn't
I won't leave you
I'll never cause you any pain

I know you can hurt me
I know I can hurt you
But I wont

You can't do anything to me
That I haven't done to someone else

-Griezelda L. May 1984

"UNTITLED"

If the right love
Comes at the wrong time,
Make the time right
It may never come again

-Griezelda L. (Undated)

"JUST ENOUGH"

You can love someone too much
And that's not good
You get so jealous and possessive
That you eventually destroy the love

You can't love too little
You have to give it all you got
If you're afraid and apprehensive
You won't give enough love

You have to love just enough
Enough so the other person is sure
Enough so the other person doesn't feel trapped
Just enough to enjoy and hold on and
Just enough to let go

-Griezelda L. Jun 1984

"HOW"

How can you write
When you can't concentrate
How can you concentrate
When you have problems

How can you solve problems
When the world is against you
How can you fight the world
When you can't understand it

How can you understand
When it's not meant to be understood

-Griezelda L. Jul 1984

CONCLUSION

At this very moment, you are probably thinking of the drug addict in your life. You may be thinking of who you could have been and how your life would have been different. I understand and believe me it took a while to get here in fact, it was 15 years after mom died that I even began to realize this needed to be dealt with. Maybe if someone explained to me that it wasn't my fault and there was nothing I could do about it, I would have dealt with life differently. maybe if the world addressed the children as a something else instead of a lost cause, I would have been okay. There are a lot of maybes, I'm sure you have some of your own, but hopefully this helps.

There are things in these short pages that at one time embarrassed me but admitting to them were vital to my growth. It is said that faith makes things possible, not easy. My faith that there was something bigger and better for me, kept me going.

If you are on your own forgiveness journey when it comes to drug addiction, this is what I would tell you.

1. Admit that you are hurt, and your feelings are valid

2. Realize that the person who did the drugs weren't born that way and more than likely something lead them there

3. Know that there is/was nothing you could have done to stop them from doing drugs

4. Think about who they were in those moments before the drugs or between them getting high

5. Focus on the good times and what they did give you rather than what they took away

6. Build off that, build you off the "new" eyes

The intention of this book is to put a face on the nameless children of drug addicts. For them to know they are not alone and are not destined to become a "product of their environment." Please understand that at the end of the day life sometime isn't fair, but that it is your choice to either fall or fly. "You don't drown by staying in the water, you drown by staying there."-Edwin Louis Cole

If you are in addiction or in recovery, please consider getting help. You can never get too far to turn around. Your children and those who love you, will forgive you and walk with you on your journey.

Thank you for reading!

-- Valencia Griffin-Wallace

CPSIA information can be obtained
at www.ICGtesting.com
Printed in the USA
LVHW080331220219
608422LV00009B/139/P